This Book
Belongs to:
Alexis
LeBlanc
W9-BFS-889

A NEW BURLINGTON BOOK
The Old Brewery
6 Blundell Street
London N7 9BH

Consultant: Fiona Moss, RE Adviser at RE Today Services
Editor: Cathy Jones
Designer: Chris Fraser

First published in the United States in 2013 by
Part of The Quarto Group
QEB Publishing
6 Orchard, Lake Forest, CA 92630

www.qed-publishing.co.uk

A CIP record for this book is available from the Library of Congress.

ISBN 978 1 60992 575 8

Printed in China

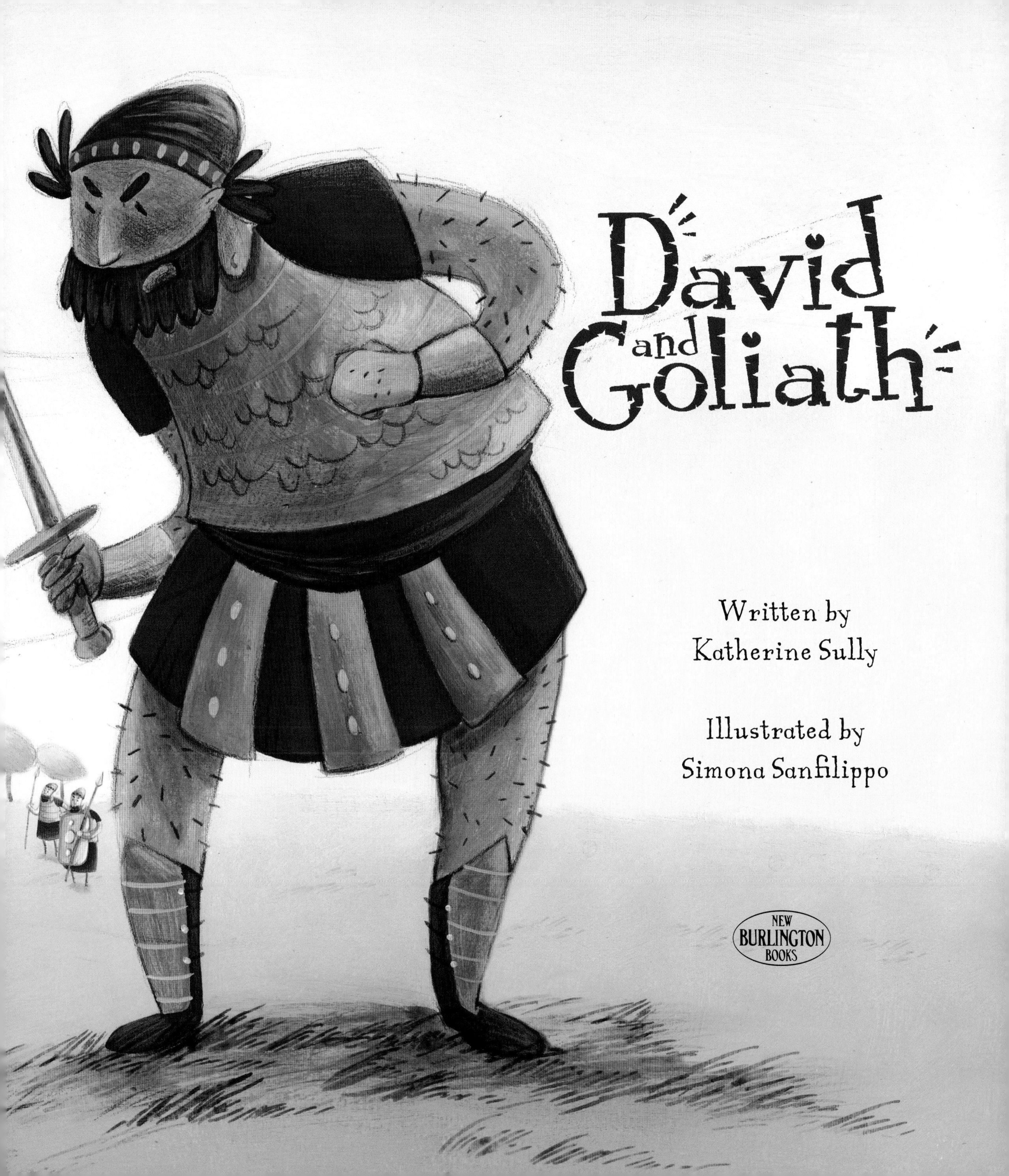

David and Goliath

Written by
Katherine Sully

Illustrated by
Simona Sanfilippo

NEW BURLINGTON BOOKS

One day, young David was looking after the sheep when he heard his father calling.

"Take this bread and cheese to your brothers," said his father. David's three older brothers were away fighting in King Saul's army.

Taking the bundle, David set off at once.

King Saul's army was camped on a hillside.
On the other hillside, the Philistine army had gathered.

It was an amazing sight!

David searched among the lines of Saul's soldiers. He soon found his three brothers.

Just then, a giant soldier stepped forward
from the Philistine army.

He was so tall,
he towered over
everyone else!

He roared:
"I am Goliath, tall and mighty.
Who is brave enough to fight me?"

Not one of King Saul's soldiers replied.
They were all afraid!

The soldiers talked among themselves.

“The king will give a big prize to whoever kills the mighty giant Goliath,” they said.

"What's going on?" young David asked his brothers.

"It has nothing to do with you," they said. "You're just a boy. Go home and look after the sheep."

But David did not go home.
He went to see King Saul in his tent.
"I will fight the giant," said David.

"I have killed a lion and a bear that tried
to attack my sheep," said David. "I was not
afraid, because God looked after me."
"But you're
just a boy, and
he is a mighty
giant!" said
the king.

King Saul gave David a helmet, armor, and a sword.
David put them on. They were much too big!
He tried walking around the tent.
"I can't wear these," he said. "I'm not used to them."
Clink!
Clank!

He took them off.

Instead, David took his sling and his pouch and went down to the stream.

There he found five smooth stones and put them in his pouch.

"My sling was all I needed to fight the lion and the bear," he thought. "God will look after me."

David went down to meet Goliath.
The giant towered over him. He roared:

"I am Goliath, tall and mighty.
Who is brave enough to fight me?"

"I am!" answered David.
"Will you fight me with that stick?"
sneered Goliath.

Goliath was angry!

Goliath lumbered toward David.

David grabbed a stone from his pouch and put it in his sling.

Goliath waved his sword in the air.

David let the stone fly through the air.

The stone hit Goliath in the middle of his forehead. He crashed to the ground.

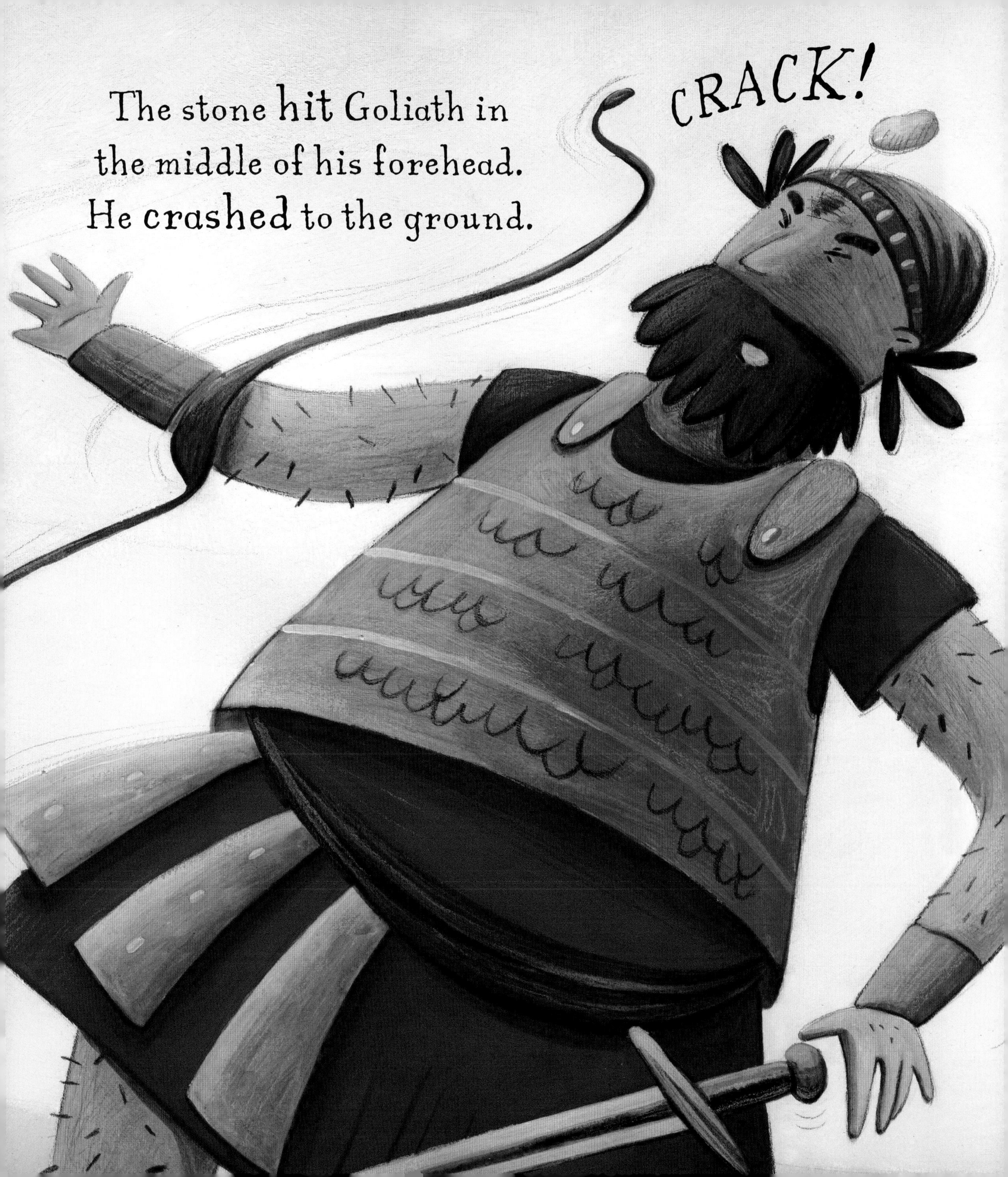

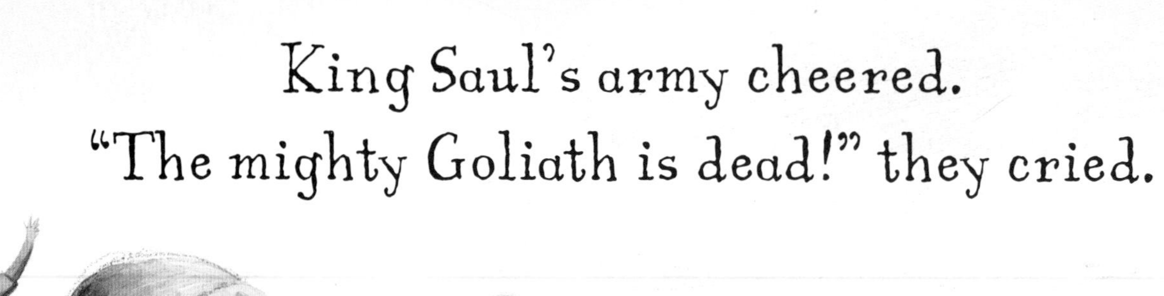

King Saul's army cheered.
"The mighty Goliath is dead!" they cried.

The Philistine army ran away,

chased by King Saul's soldiers.

Young David was a hero!

Next Steps

Look back through the book to find more to talk about and join in with.

* Make yourself big and tall. Make yourself small and short. Pretend you are throwing a shot from a sling. Pretend you have a sword.
* Join in with the rhyme. Pause to encourage joining in with, "I am Goliath, tall and mighty. Who is brave enough to fight me?"
* Count three brothers. Goliath is 9 feet (3 meters) tall. Talk about how high that is—as tall as a basketball hoop, or an elephant.
* Name the colors of the tents. Look back through the book to spot the colors on other pages.
* Find shapes and sizes. Describe the armor that Goliath is wearing. Use words like hard, stiff, shiny, metal, leather.
* Listen to the sounds. When you see the word on the page, point and make the sound—Clink! Clank! Crack!

Now that you've read the story...what do you remember?

* Who was David?
* Why did he go to find his brothers?
* Where did David find King Saul?
* What happened when David tried on the armor?
* How did David have the strength to fight Goliath?
* Why did Goliath crash to the ground?

What does the story tell us?
We can face big problems if God is on our side.